BIG-NOTE PIANO

Gospel Time

CONTENTS

2 Amazing Grace

4 At Calvary

10 Blessed Redeemer

7 Do Lord

12 Does Jesus Care?

18 Down at the Cross

20 Give Me That Old Time Religion

15 God Will Take Care of You

22 Higher Ground

24 I Feel Like Traveling On

26 I Have Decided to Follow Jesus

28 I've Got Peace Like a River

30 Jesus Is the Sweetest Name I Know

36 Just Over in the Gloryland

38 The Love of God

33 A New Name in Glory

46 Precious Memories

40 Send the Light

42 Since Jesus Came into My Heart

44 Sweet By and By

ISBN 0-634-01271-1

HAL•LEONARD®
CORPORATION

7777 W. BLUEMOUND RD. P.O. BOX 13819 MILWAUKEE, WI 53213

Visit Hal Leonard Online at
www.halleonard.com

AMAZING GRACE

Words by JOHN NEWTON
Traditional American Melody

Moderately

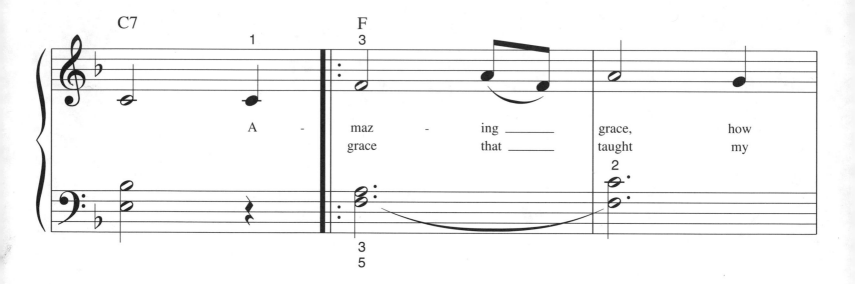

A - maz - ing _____ grace, how
grace that _____ taught my

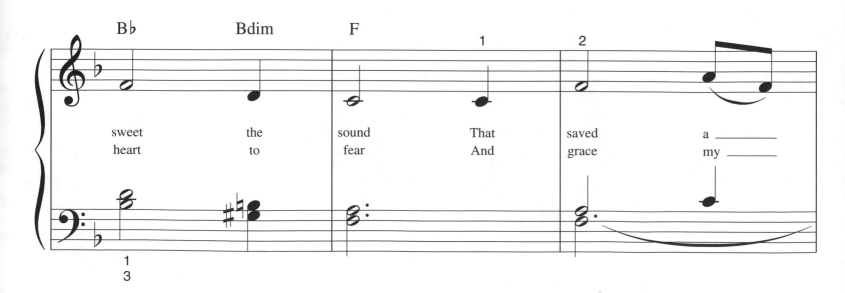

sweet the sound That saved a _____
heart to fear And grace my _____

AT CALVARY

Words by WILLIAM NEWELL
Music by D.B. TOWNER

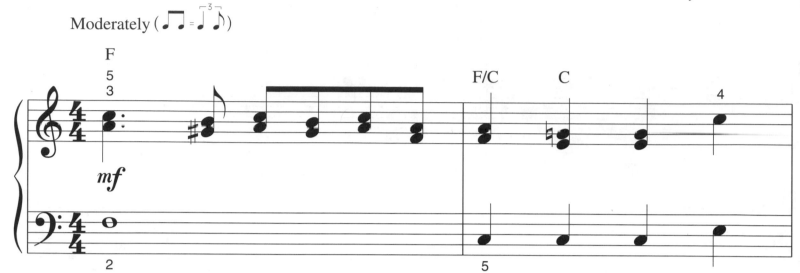

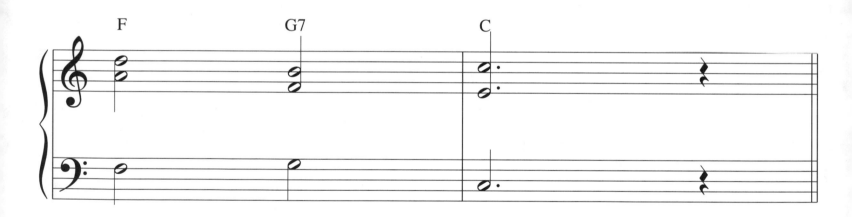

1. Years   I   spent   in   van - i - ty   and   pride,
2. Now   I've   giv'n   to   Je - sus   ev - 'ry - thing,
3. Oh,   the   love   that   drew   sal - va - tion's   plan!
4. *(See additional verse)*

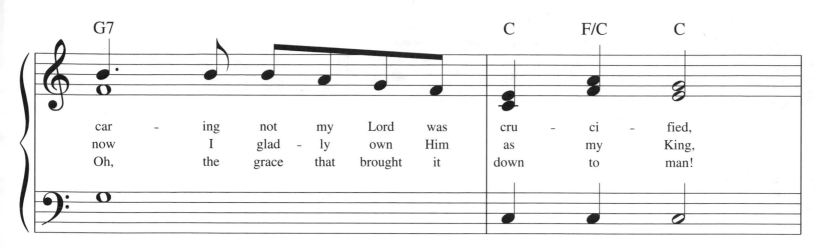

car - ing not my Lord was | cru - ci - fied,
now I glad - ly own Him | as my King,
Oh, the grace that brought it | down to man!

know - ing not it was for | me He died on
now my rap - tured soul can | on - ly sing of
Oh, the might - y gulf that | God did span at

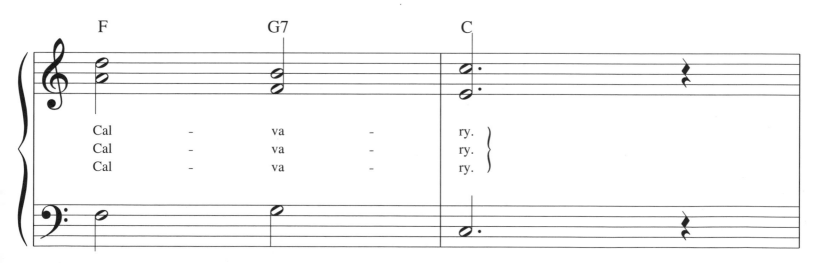

Cal - va - ry.
Cal - va - ry.
Cal - va - ry.

Refrain

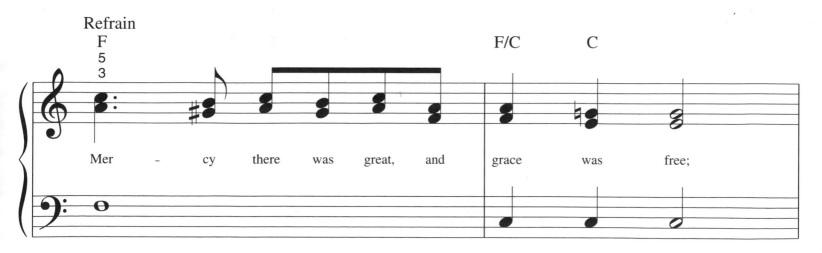

Mer - cy there was great, and | grace was free;

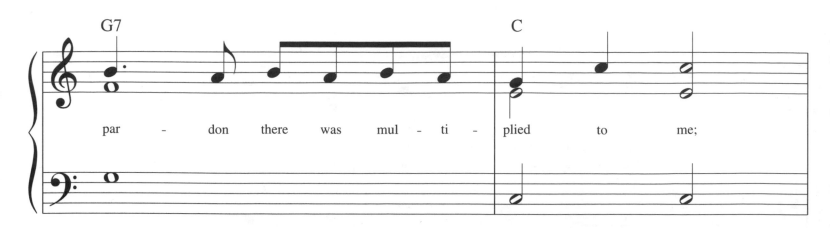

par - don there was mul - ti - plied to me;

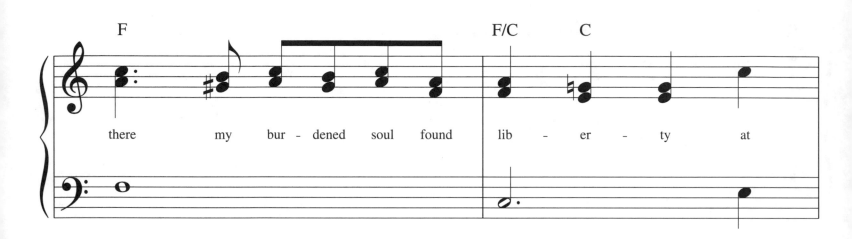

there my bur - dened soul found lib - er - ty at

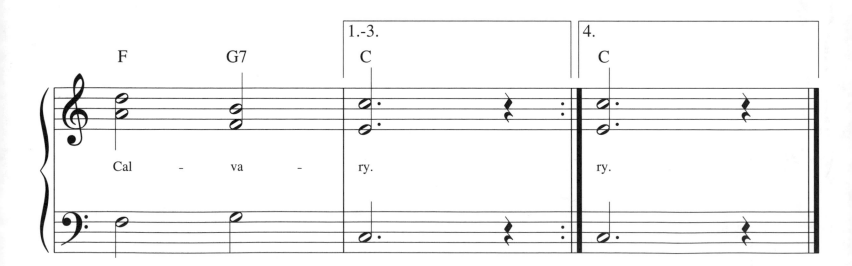

Cal - va - ry. ry.

Additional Verse

4. By God's Word at last my sin I learned;
Then I trembled at the law I'd spurned,
Till my guilty soul imploring turned to Calvary.
Refrain

DO LORD

Traditional

Moderately fast

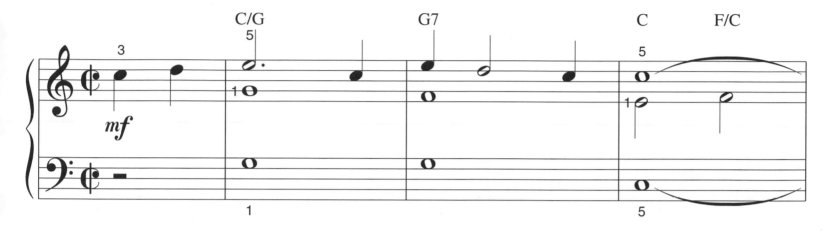

I've got a home in glory land that out-shines the
I took Je - sus as my Sav - ior, you take Him

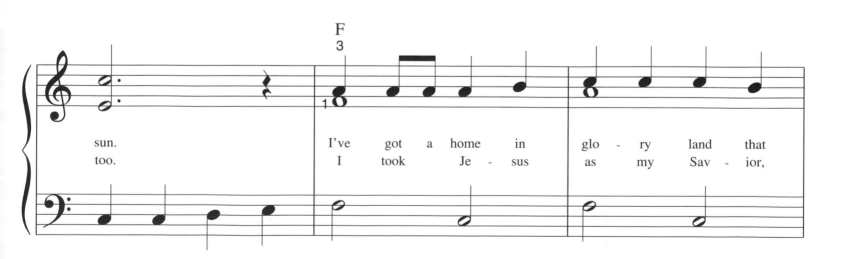

sun.
too.

I've got a home in glory land that
I took Je - sus as my Sav - ior,

out - shines the sun.
you take the Him too.

I've got a home in
I took Je - sus

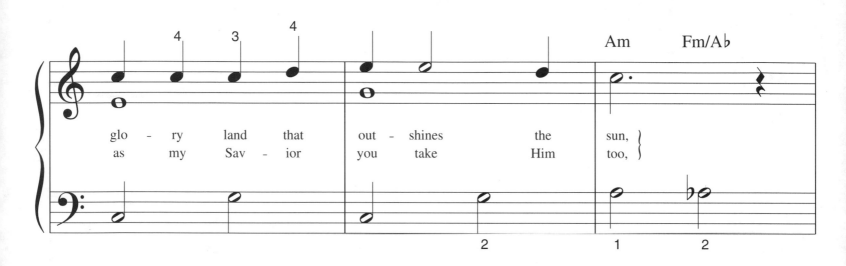

glo - ry land that
as my Sav - ior

out - shines the sun,
you take the Him too, }

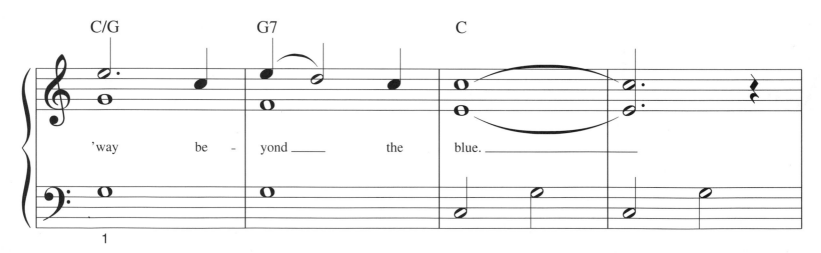

'way be - yond ____ the blue. ____

Do Lord, oh, do Lord, oh do re - mem - ber

BLESSED REDEEMER

Words by AVIS B. CHRISTIANSEN
Music by HARRY DIXON LOES

DOES JESUS CARE?

Words by FRANK E. GRAEFF
Music by J. LINCOLN HALL

Moderately slow

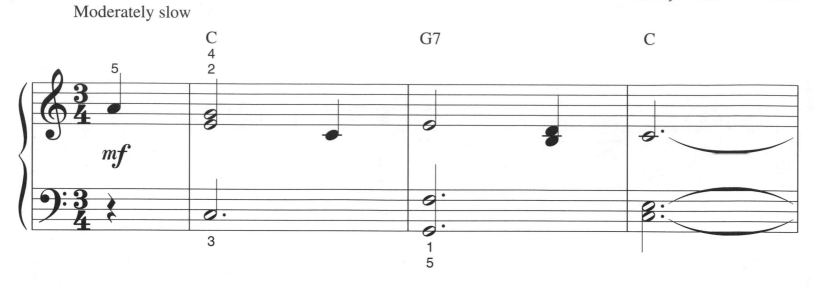

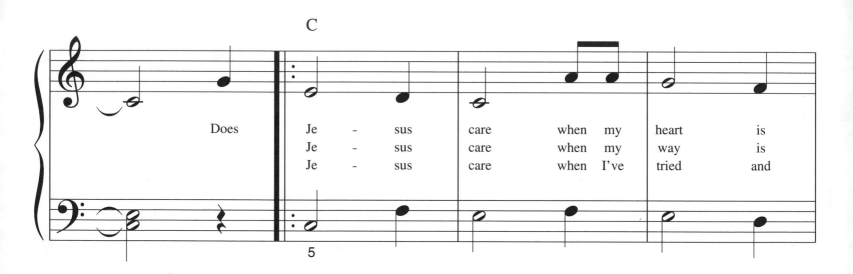

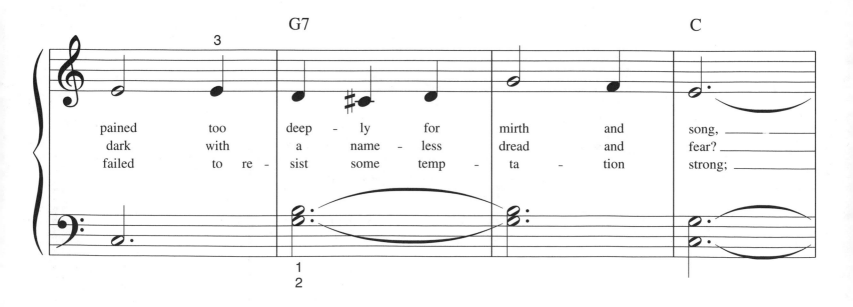

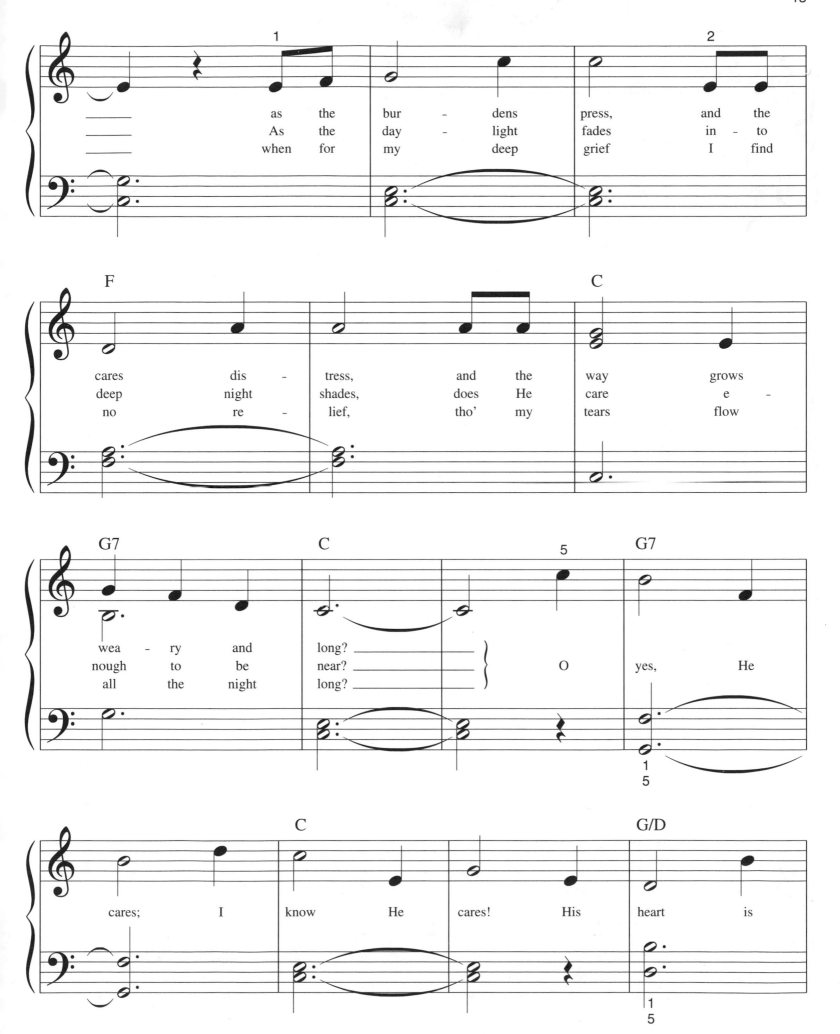

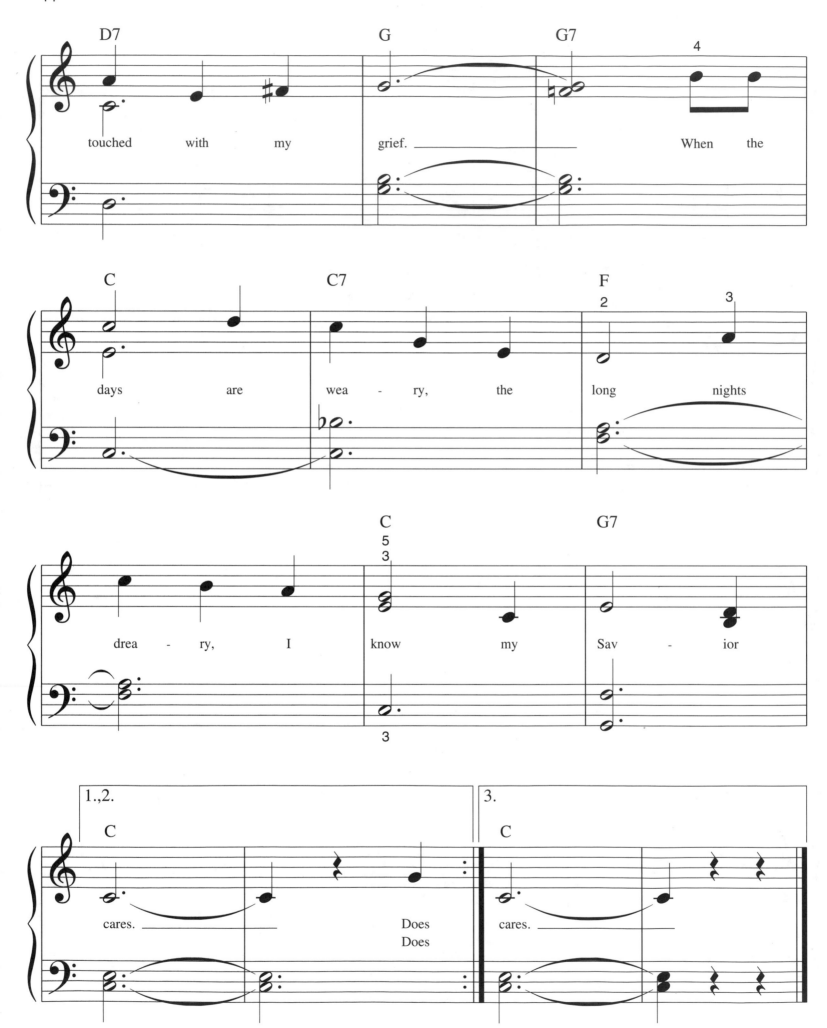

GOD WILL TAKE CARE OF YOU

Words by CIVILLA D. MARTIN
Music by W. STILLMAN MARTIN

Moderately

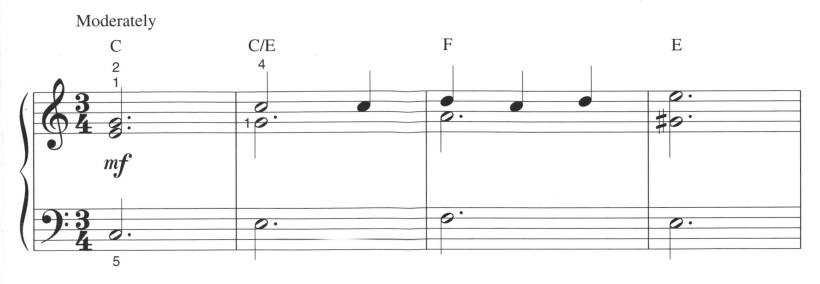

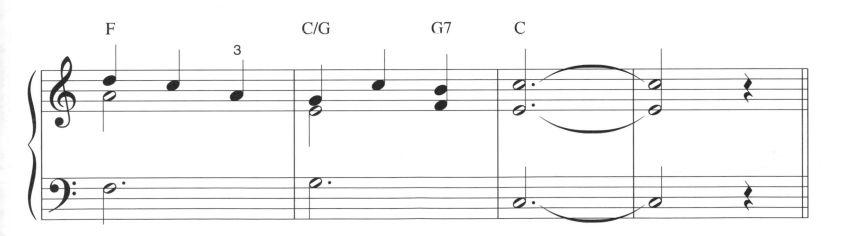

Be not dis - mayed what - e'er be -
Through days of toil when heart doth
All you may need He will pro -

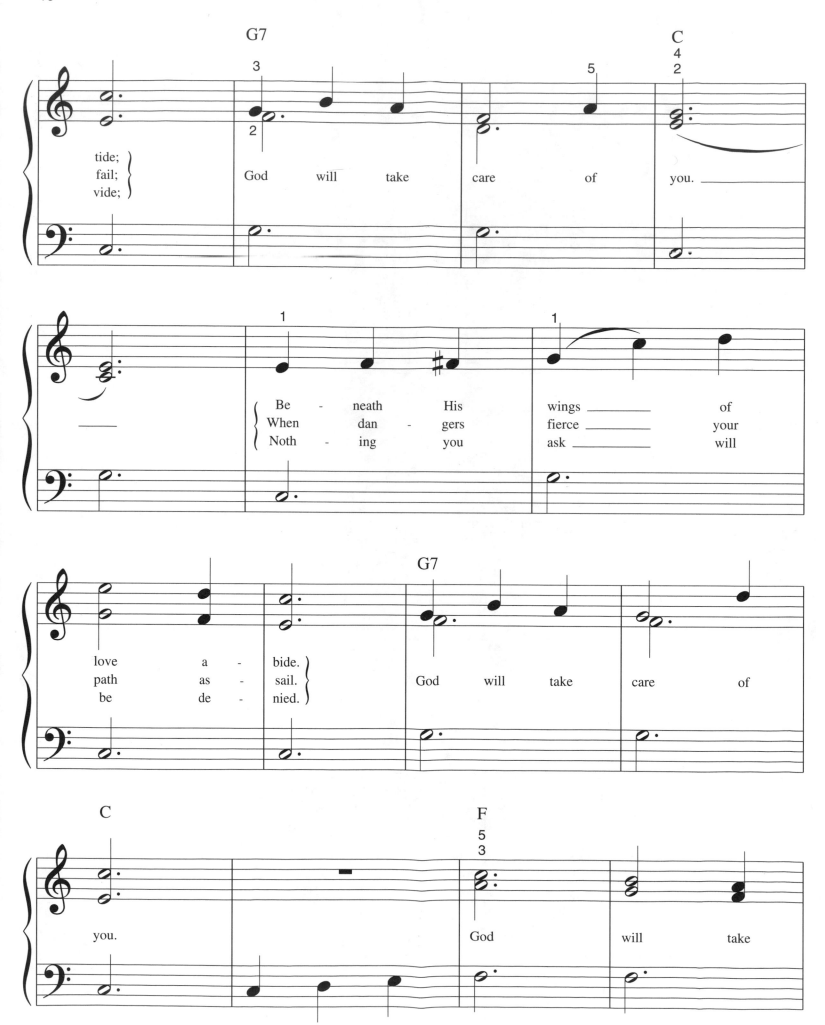

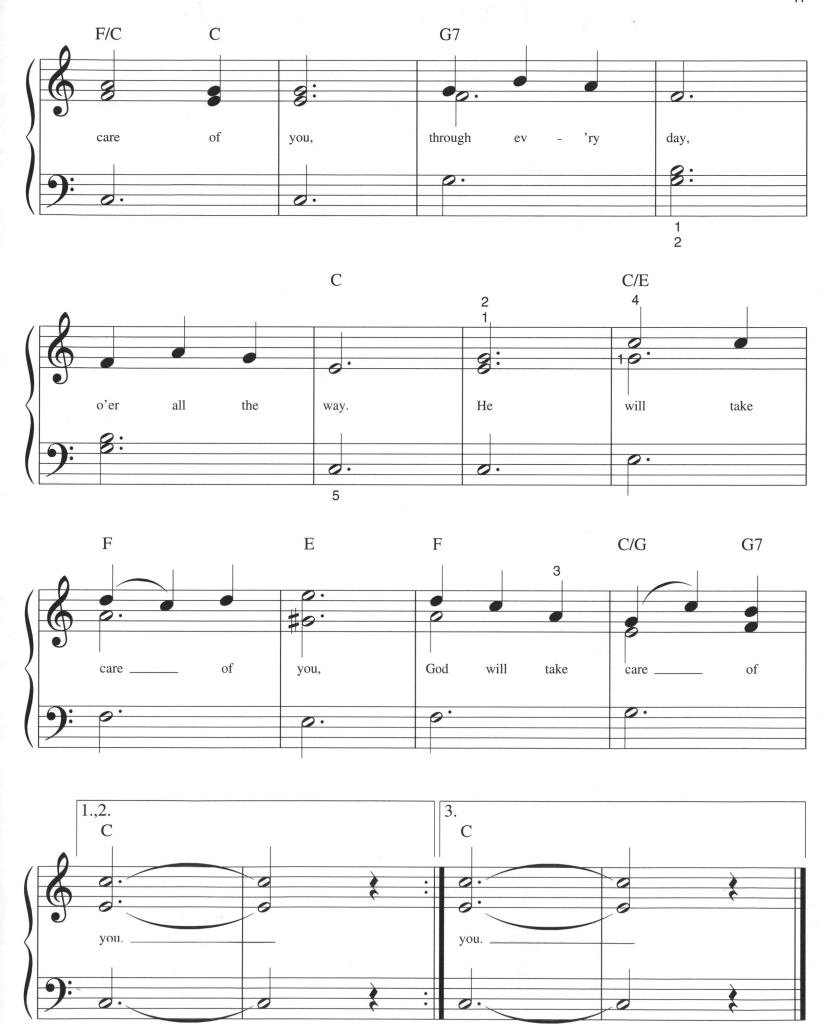

DOWN AT THE CROSS

Words by ELISHA A. HOFFMAN
Music by JOHN H. STOCKTON

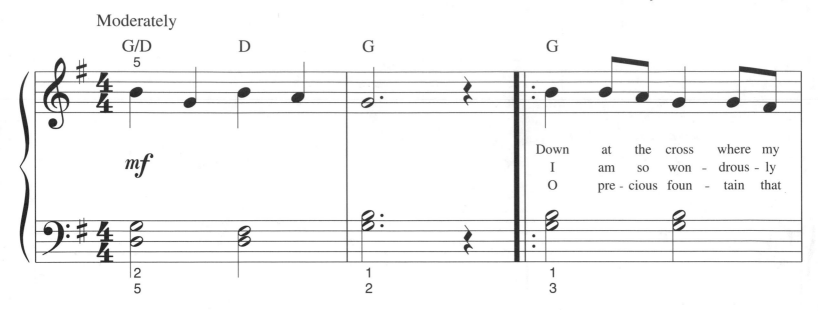

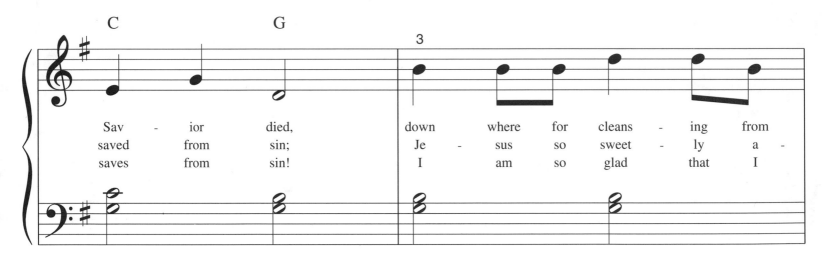

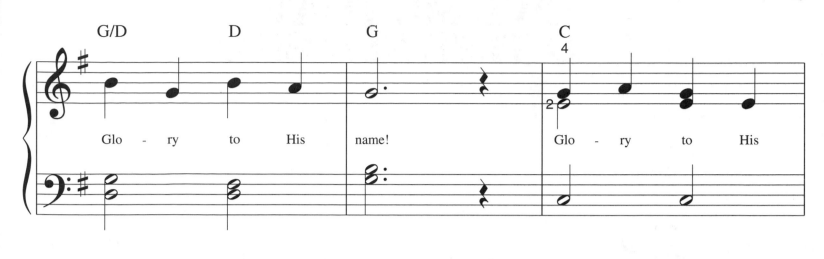

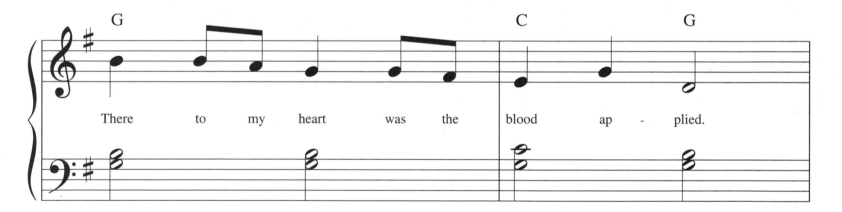

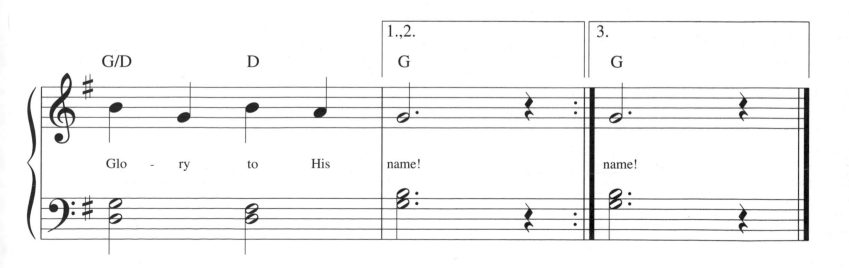

GIVE ME THAT OLD TIME RELIGION

Traditional

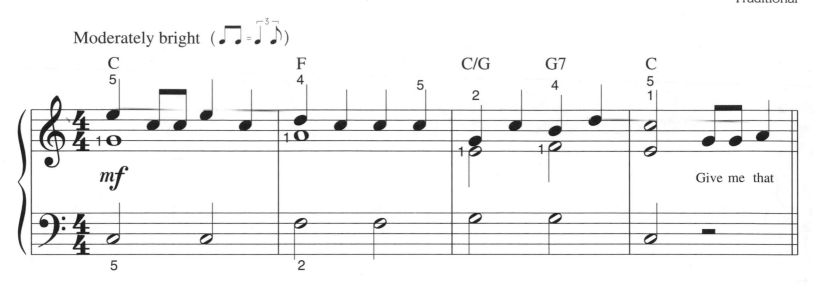

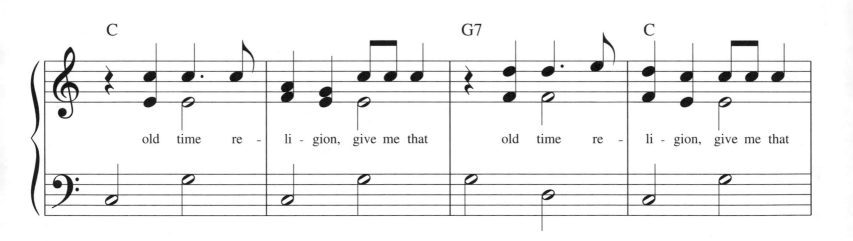

good for the proph - et Dan - iel, it was
good for Paul and Si - las, it was

good for the proph - et Dan - iel, it was
good for Paul and Si - las, it was

good for the proph - et Dan - iel and it's good e - nough for me.}
good for Paul and Si - las and it's good e - nough for me.}

Give me that

old time re - li - gion, give me that old time re - li - gion, give me that

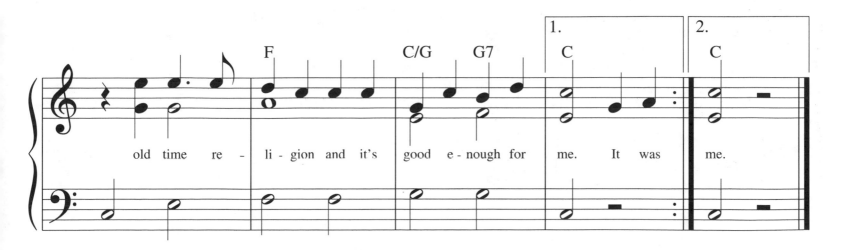

old time re - li - gion and it's good e - nough for me. It was me.

HIGHER GROUND

Words by JOHNSON OATMAN, JR.
Music by CHARLES H. GABRIEL

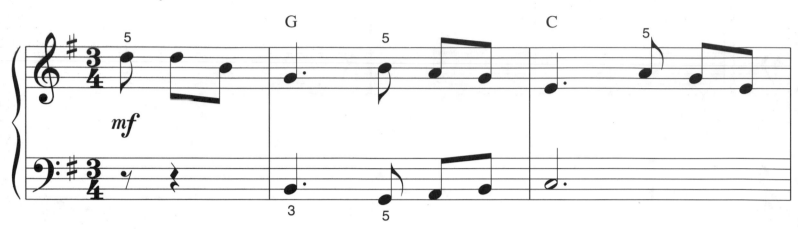

I'm press - ing on the up - ward
live a - bove the
scale the ut - most

way, new heights I'm gain - ing ev - 'ry day; still pray - ing
world, tho Sa - tan's darts at me are hurled; for faith has
height, and catch a gleam of glo - ry bright; but still I'll

I FEEL LIKE TRAVELING ON

Words by WILLIAM HUNTER
Anonymous Music
Music arranged by JAMES D. VAUGHAN

Moderately

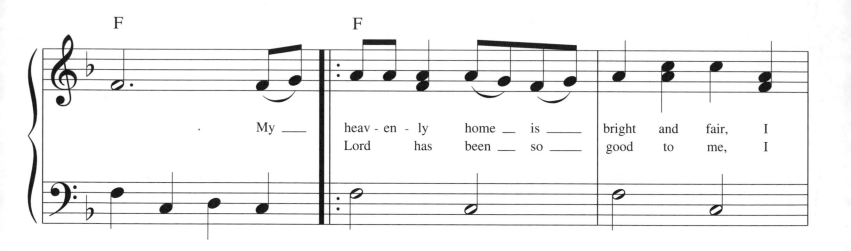

My ___ heav - en - ly home ___ is ___ bright and fair, I
Lord has been ___ so ___ good to me, I

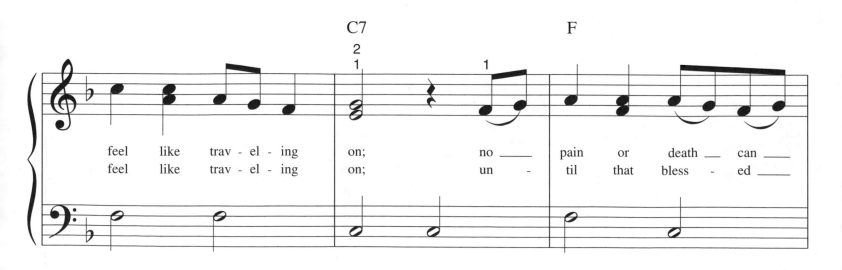

feel like trav - el - ing on; no ___ pain or death ___ can ___
feel like trav - el - ing on; un - til that bless - ed ___

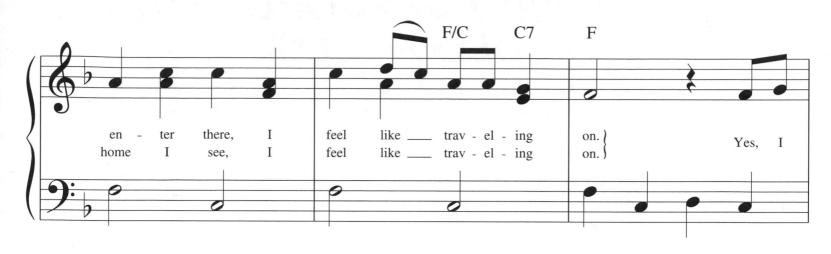

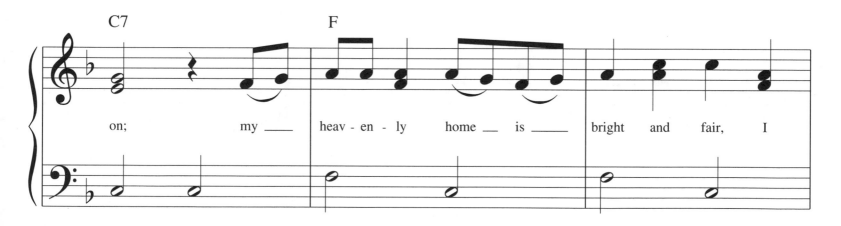

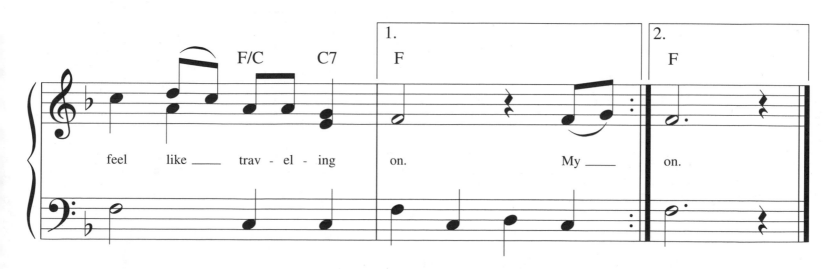

I HAVE DECIDED
TO FOLLOW JESUS

Words by an Indian Prince
Music by AUILA READ

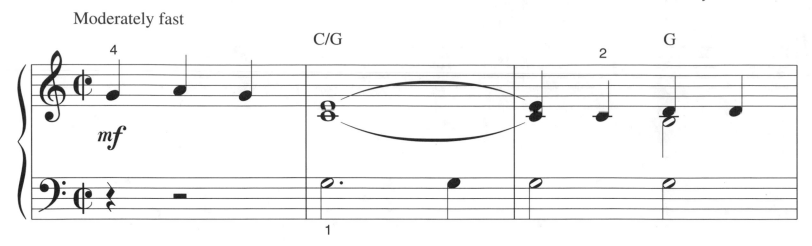

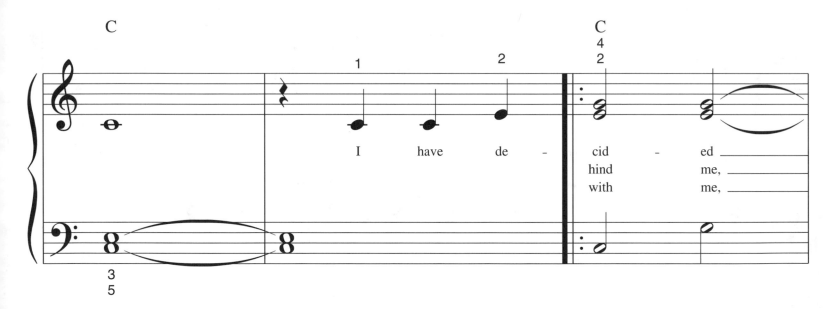

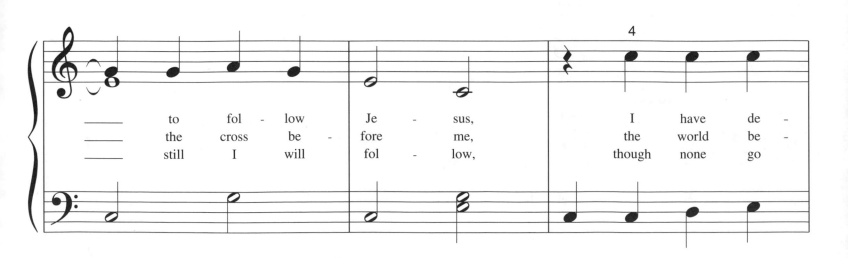

27

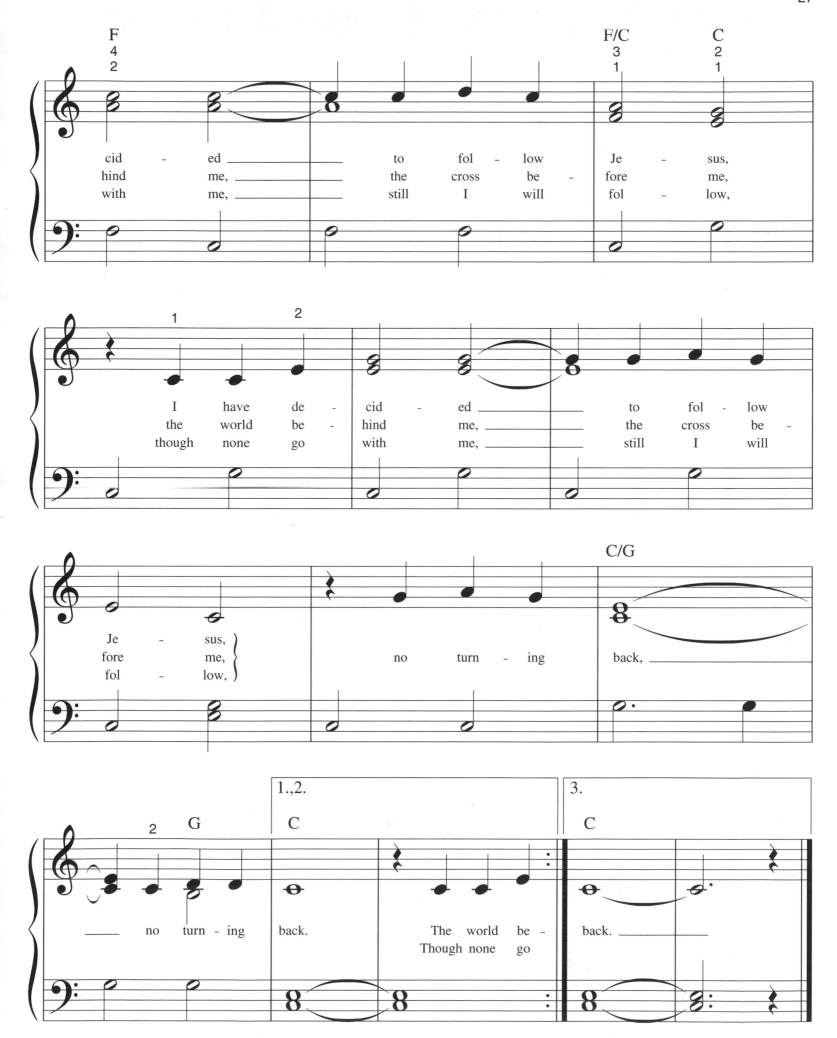

I'VE GOT PEACE LIKE A RIVER

Traditional

Moderately slow

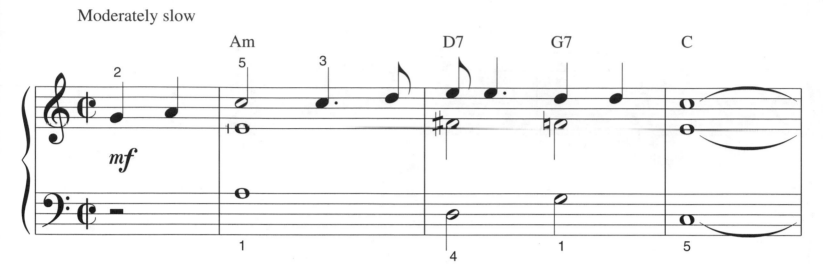

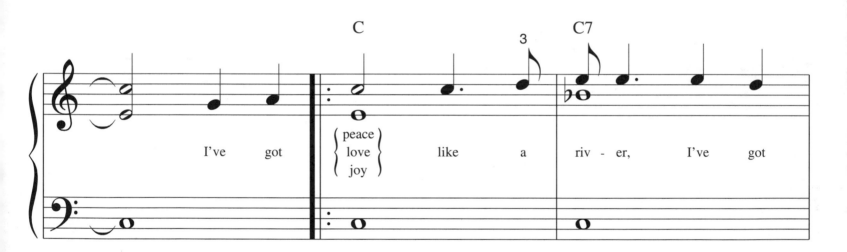

I've got peace/love/joy like a river, I've got

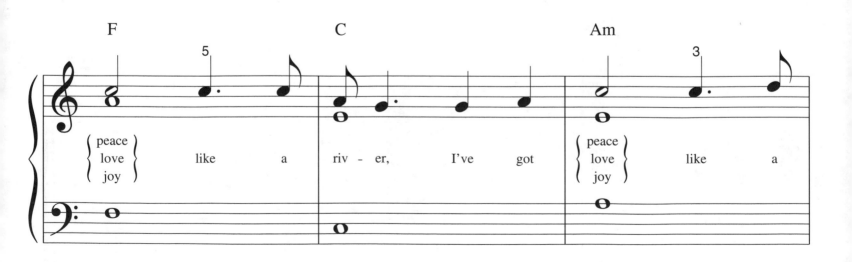

peace/love/joy like a river, I've got peace/love/joy like a

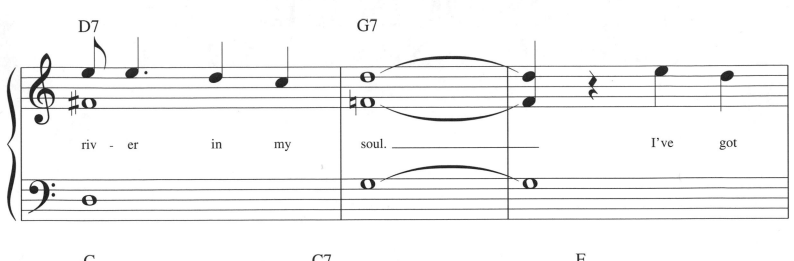

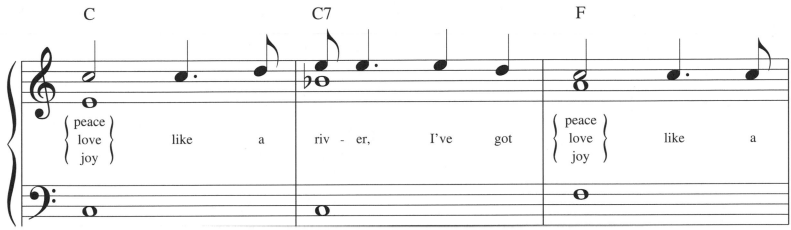

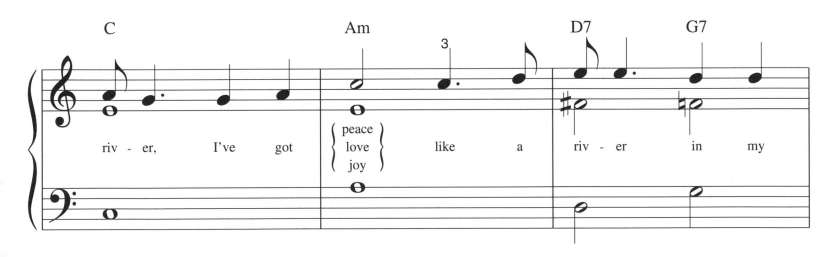

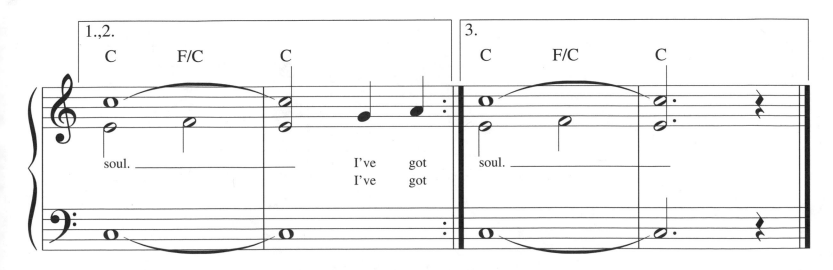

JESUS IS THE SWEETEST NAME I KNOW

Words and Music by
LELA LONG

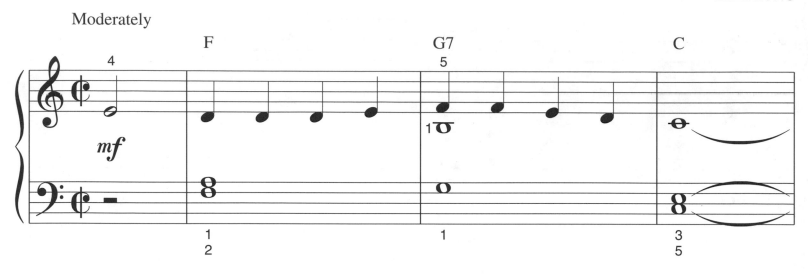

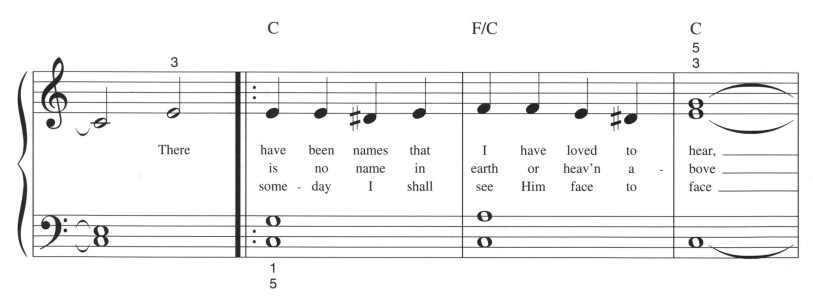

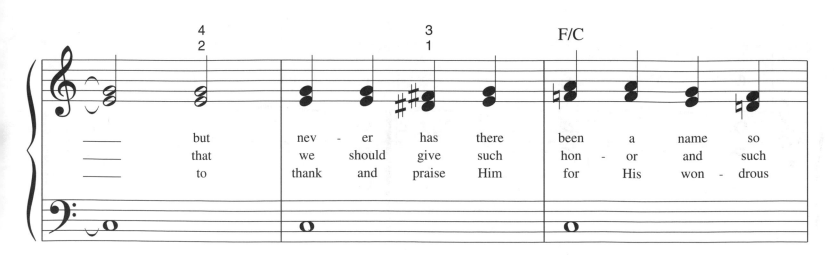

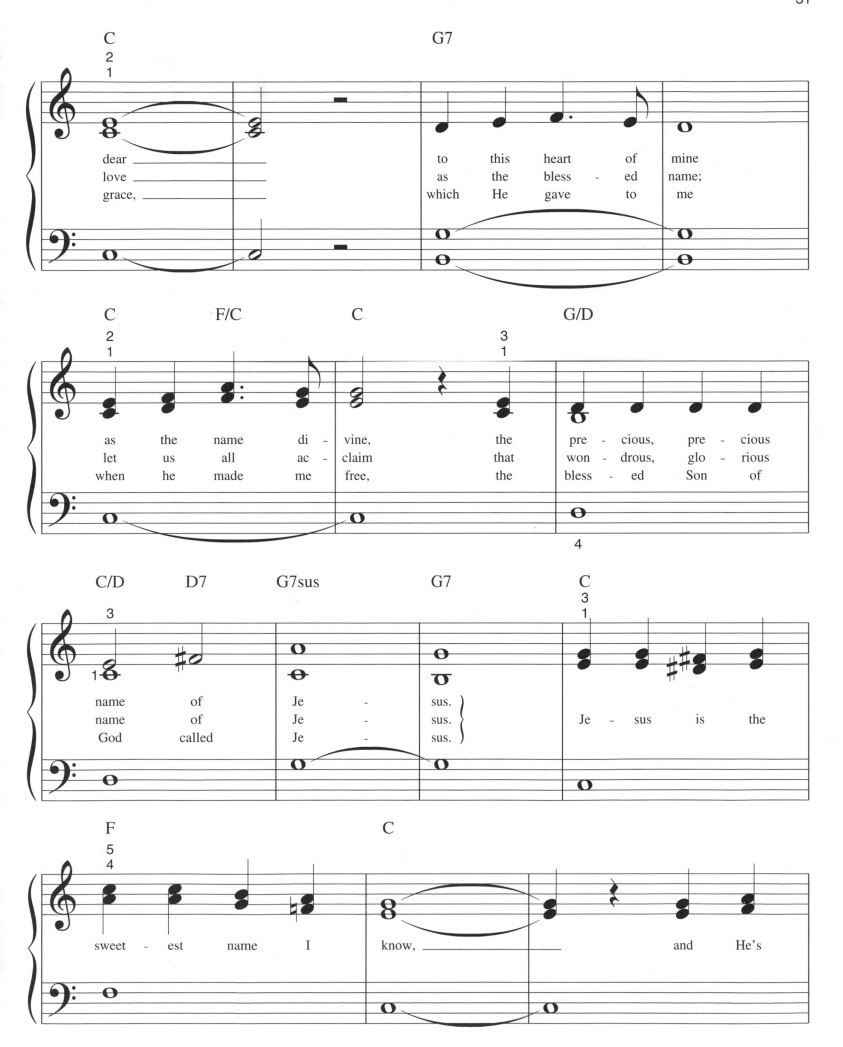

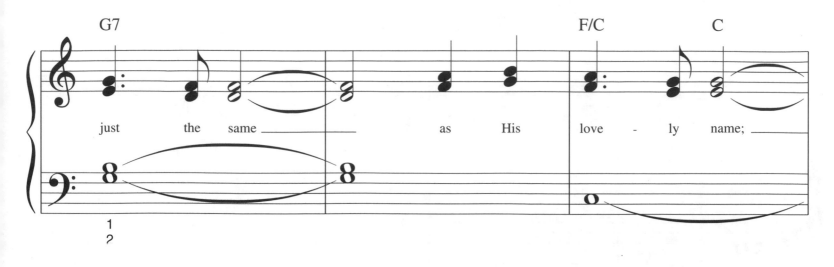

just the same _____ as His love - ly name; _____

_____ and that's the rea - son why I love Him

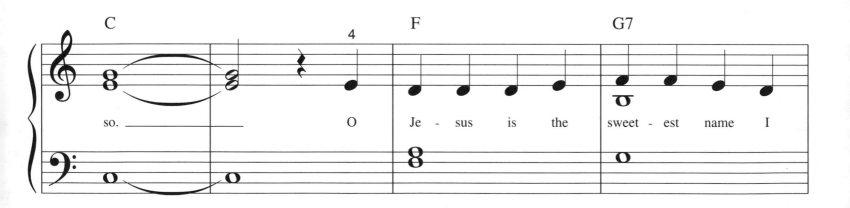

so. _____ O Je - sus is the sweet - est name I

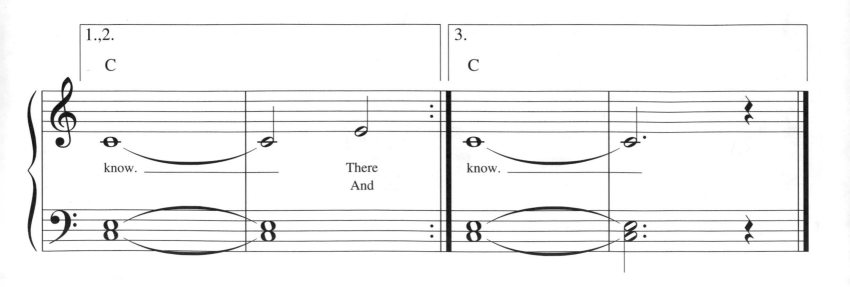

1.,2. know. _____ There
And

3. know. _____

A NEW NAME IN GLORY

Words and Music by
C. AUSTIN MILES

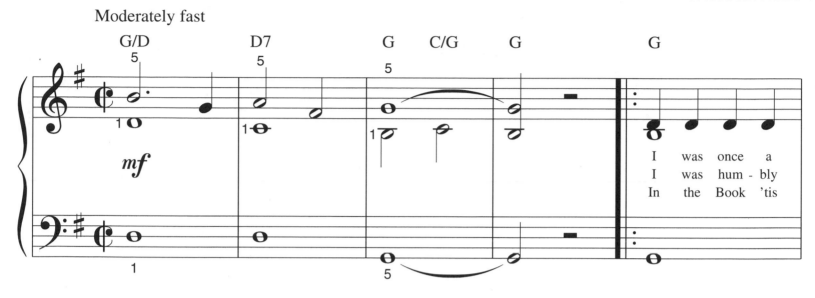

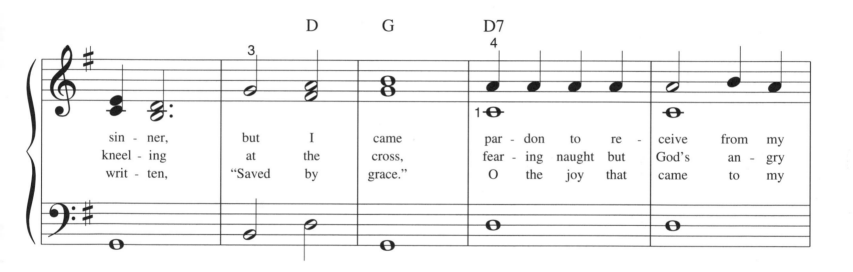

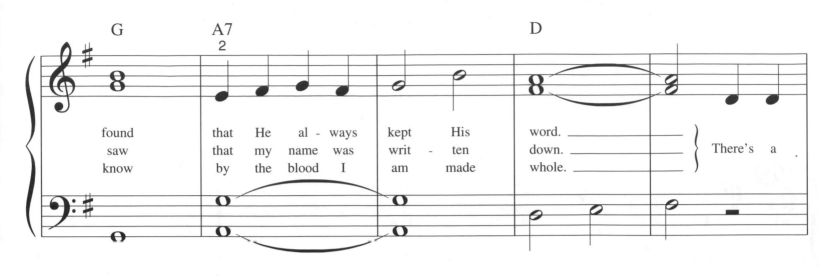

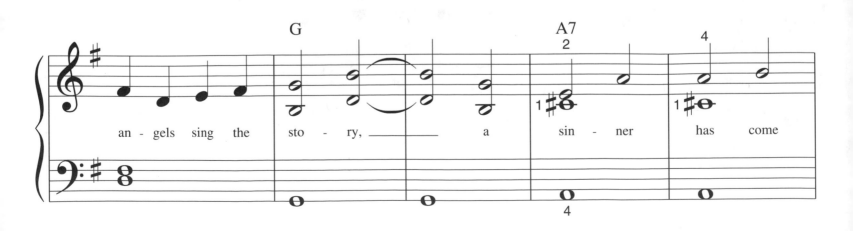

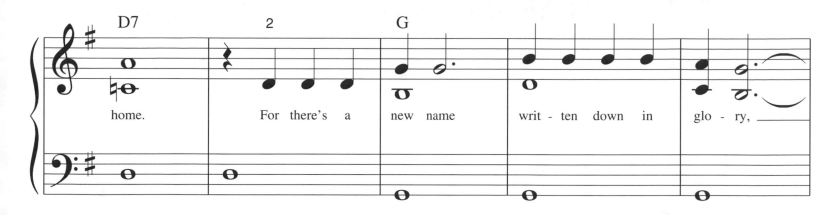

home. For there's a new name writ - ten down in glo - ry, ____

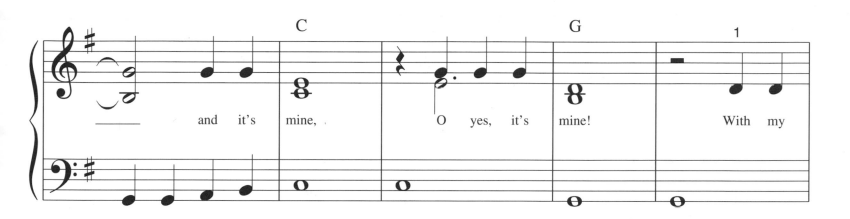

____ and it's mine, O yes, it's mine! With my

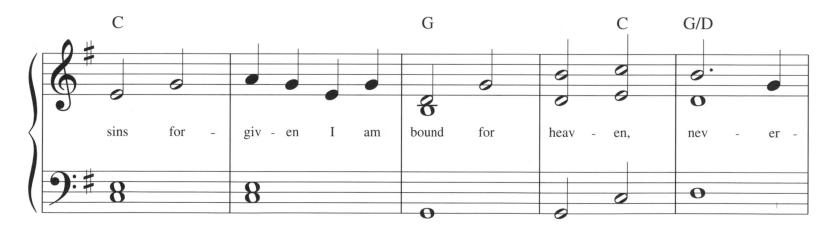

sins for - giv - en I am bound for heav - en, nev - er -

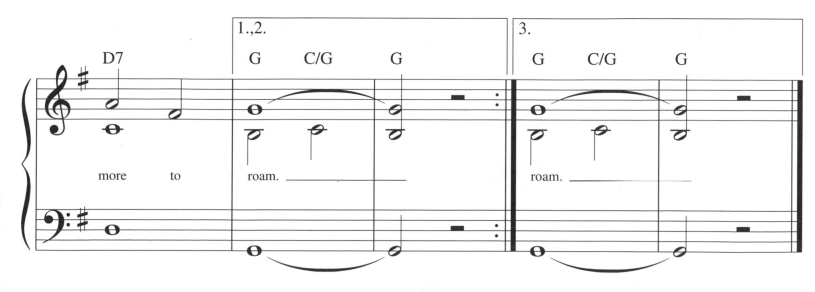

more to roam. ____ roam. ____

JUST OVER IN THE GLORYLAND

Words and Music by J.W. ACUFF
and EMMETT DEAN

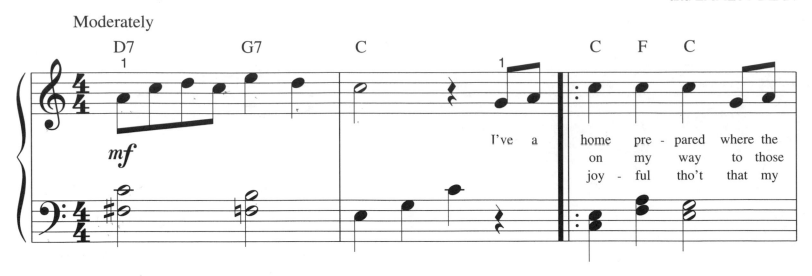

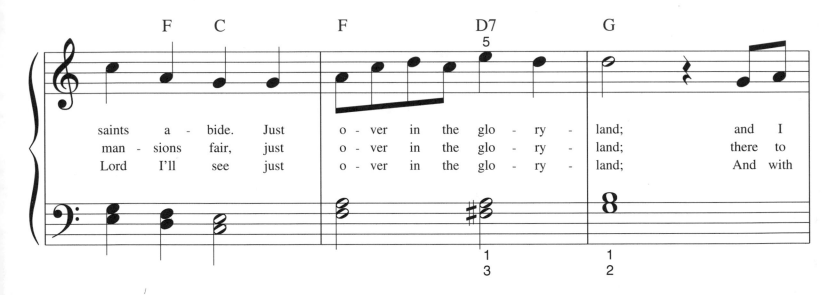

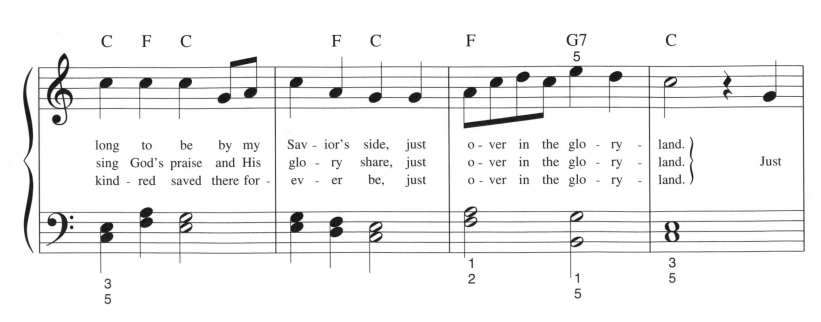

THE LOVE OF GOD

Words and Music by
FREDERICK M. LEHMAN

Moderately

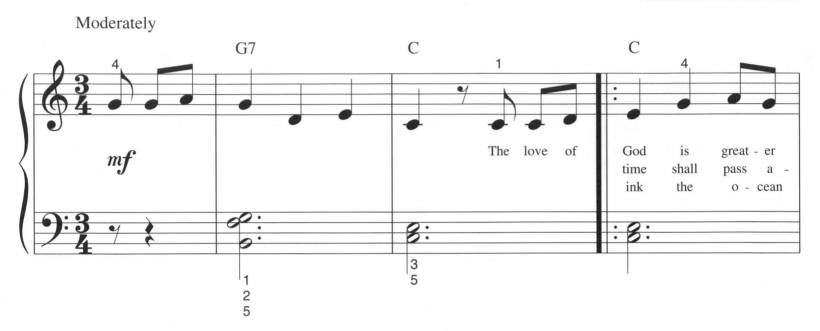

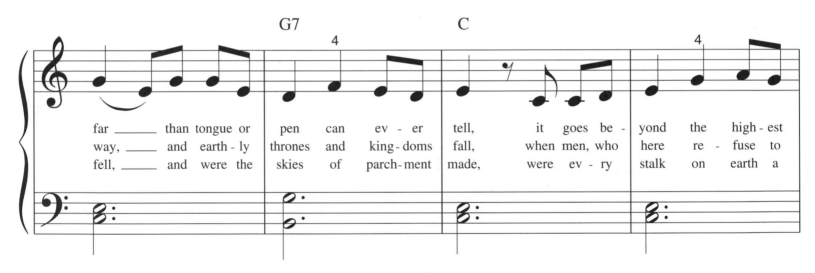

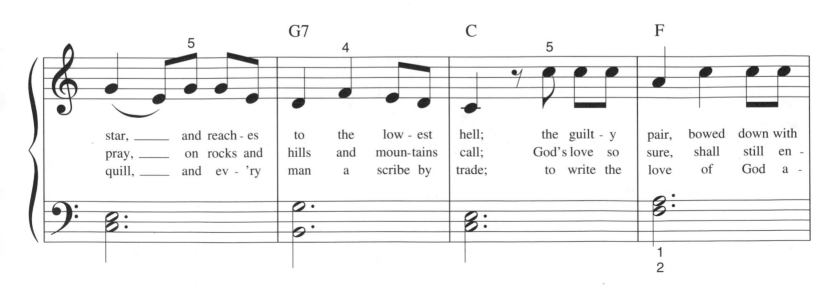

SEND THE LIGHT

Words and Music by
CHARLES GABRIEL

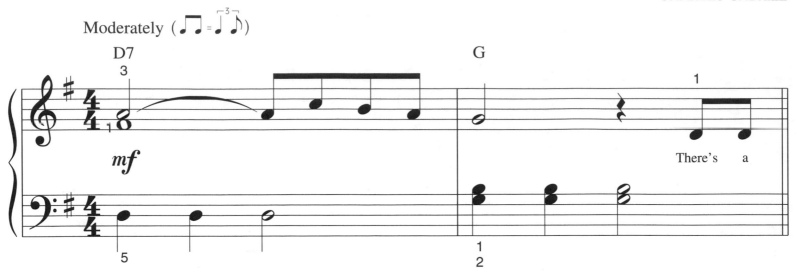

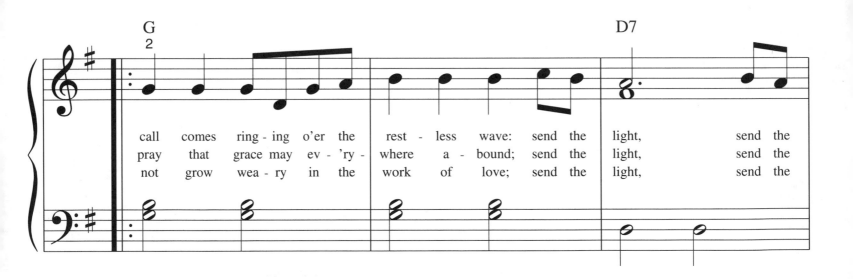

SINCE JESUS CAME INTO MY HEART

Words by R.H. McDANIEL
Music by CHARLES H. GABRIEL

Moderately fast

won - der - ful change in my life has been wrought, since
sessed of a hope that is stead - fast and sure, since

Je - sus came in - to my heart! I have light in my soul for which
Je - sus came in - to my heart! And no dark clouds of doubt now my

SWEET BY AND BY

Words by SANFORD FILLMORE BENNETT
Music by JOSEPH P. WEBSTER

45

PRECIOUS MEMORIES

Words and Music by
J.B.F. WRIGHT